$\mathcal{S}$ucceeding *in the* Inclusive Classroom

K–12 Lesson Plans Using Universal Design for Learning

Debbie Metcalf

East Carolina University

Pitt County Schools, Greenville, North Carolina

Los Angeles | London | New Delhi
Singapore | Washington DC

For information:

SAGE Publications, Inc.
2455 Teller Road
Thousand Oaks, California 91320
E-mail: order@sagepub.com

SAGE Publications Ltd.
1 Oliver's Yard
55 City Road
London EC1Y 1SP
United Kingdom

SAGE Publications India Pvt. Ltd.
B 1/I 1 Mohan Cooperative Industrial Area
Mathura Road, New Delhi 110 044
India

SAGE Publications Asia-Pacific Pte. Ltd.
33 Pekin Street #02-01
Far East Square
Singapore 048763

Printed in the United States of America on acid-free paper.

10 11 12 13 14   10 9 8 7 6 5 4 3 2 1

Acquisitions Editor:	Diane McDaniel
Editorial Assistant:	Ashley Conlon
Production Editor:	Laureen Gleason
Typesetter:	C&M Digitals (P) Ltd.
Proofreader:	Vicki Reed-Castro
Cover Designer:	Candice Harman

Contents

Preface

*S*ucceeding in the Inclusive Classroom: K–12 Lesson Plans Using Universal Design for Learning* has been designed to help K–12 teachers think about ways to apply the principles of Universal Design for Learning (UDL) in planning. With the growing diversity of learners in 21st-century schools and legislative mandates for accountability and standards-based instruction for *all* students, it is critical that teachers plan for the wide range of learner needs up front to be as effective as possible.

Students come to school from many different cultural backgrounds. Some speak different languages while others simply struggle with basic communication skills. Some have sensory challenges, emotional disabilities, and other exceptional needs that require adaptations. Many are gifted and talented. More students today with exceptional needs are being served in general education classrooms across the country. In addition, students are more technologically savvy than ever before. Because we all learn in different ways, today's teacher must have a manageable way of adding flexibility to a lesson plan.

Most teachers, I believe, know what good teaching looks like and want the best for each learner in the classroom. Pre-service and in-service teachers are trained in traditional lesson planning formats based on sound research and development. We attend many classes or staff development activities to add to our knowledge about content area instruction, brain-based learning, co-teaching, English language learners, differentiated instruction, exceptional learners, learning styles, learning strategies, multiple intelligences, diversity, the latest in technology updates, and more. The task of lesson planning today can be overwhelming. It is a lot to process! UDL lesson planning just might be a solution.

APPROACH

The UDL lesson planning format presented here is offered as one possible way to add flexibility to a lesson plan. On the pages that follow, the tried and true elements of a traditional lesson plan format are presented with an additional layer of planning to match learner needs. It applies the three principles of UDL: multiple means of (1) representation, (2) expression, and (3) engagement. Are we presenting content in a variety of ways that match our learners' abilities to receive and perceive information? Are we thinking about incorporating a variety of strategies and products that will enable each student to show us what they know? Are we fully engaging our learners? The premise behind the application of these principles is that if we can identify the challenges or barriers our students face, then we can brainstorm ideas that will help us make learning come alive for each one of them.

This lesson planning format also links goals, objectives, and assessment up front. This practice can help teachers stay on course. All expectations are clear from the start. In addition, strategic connections are made between discipline areas when possible to help the learner see patterns and make associations in their learning. Attention to this important practice will help students develop their own overall ability to plan, organize, and apply their thinking. You will also notice that social skills are often infused with academic skills in these lesson plans to help all learners develop or reinforce prosocial competencies.

Methods, materials, and tools are important elements to consider in UDL lesson planning. Research-based learning and organization strategies, behavior management techniques, and communication methods will all need to be considered. Choosing the right materials and tools also increases a lesson plan's flexibility. These materials and tools can be both high-tech and low-tech. Examples of high-tech tools may include computers, digitized video, text-to-speech software, electronic whiteboards, and iPods. Low-tech tools can be items such as highlighters, dry erase boards, response cards, posters, drawings, or pencil grips. Many of these tools are offered as examples in these sample lesson plans.

The last step in this lesson planning format is to consider pyramid planning. Pyramid planning is a visual organizing tool that helps teachers to further differentiate instruction for all students. It may consider both product and process—what students will do and how they will do it. At the base of the pyramid, teachers think about what the essential concepts in a lesson are that *all* students will be able to learn and express. In the middle section, teachers think about what *most* students will do. Learners might be asked to extend their thinking, find more information, or vary the process of their work. In the top section, teachers think about what *some* students will do. This might include applying even more complex thinking, incidental information/adaptations that relate to the major learning goals, or varying a process to an even greater degree (i.e., creating an Excel spreadsheet instead of making a paper/pencil graph to display data).

Collaboration should enhance all of these lesson plans and is another cornerstone of UDL. If you have the opportunity to co-teach or have other adults working in the classroom, the work can be easier if you can divide up the tasks during the planning stages. Be sure to find out who can assist you from the community with resources or by volunteering. Remember, too, that other students can be valuable human resources when trained to be peer tutors, mediators, or experts in other ways using their areas of strength.

ORGANIZATION

This text consists of lesson plans that correlate with the ten disability areas addressed in Part II of Richard Gargiulo's *Special Education in Contemporary Society*. One lesson at the elementary level and one lesson at the middle school/secondary level are presented for each area of special need. These lessons are only meant to be a starting point for general and special education teachers who have students with special needs in their classrooms and can be adapted for K–12 learners with a much wider range of challenges.

The learners whose special needs are addressed in this text are:

1. Individuals with intellectual disabilities

2. Individuals with learning disabilities

3. Individuals with attention deficit hyperactivity disorder

4. Individuals with emotional or behavioral disorders

5. Individuals with autism spectrum disorders

6. Individuals with speech and language disorders

7. Individuals with hearing impairments

8. Individuals with visual impairments

9. Individuals with physical disabilities, health disabilities, and related low-incidence disabilities

10. Individuals who are gifted and talented

I chose the theme "The Olympics: Past, Present, and Future" to anchor these sample lesson plans for two reasons. First, the content is timely and relevant; these are events that students can likely relate to. Second, it is a "big idea" from an interdisciplinary area (social studies) that gives students the opportunity to explore the characteristics of people who set goals, solve problems, show determination, and persevere. Infusing learning with these core values and characteristics can be inspiring to all students and help them think about making better choices in their own lives.

State standards for North Carolina were used to guide these lesson plans but they can easily be adapted for other states. The plans are simply presented to be used as a springboard for developing your own UDL lessons. In practice, you will likely need to consider all learner barriers on one plan rather than just one disability area.

MAKING THESE LESSON PLANS YOUR OWN

In conclusion, as a teacher and teacher trainer, I have taught and observed many lessons about the Olympics and related topics. It is difficult to have an "original" lesson although we all have our own unique "stamp" on what we do. It is likely some of you have written or observed content that is similar to these sample plans. The focus of my work with them is on the UDL components rather than on the lesson components. In most cases, I have only sketched out the lesson elements in order to illustrate possible UDL applications. I encourage you to try the same technique to see how you can build upon your own lessons so that they can work more effectively for students with a variety of different learning needs. You will add your own unique detailing and personal "stamp." It is my hope that the sample lesson plan format included in this text will provide you with another tool you can use to design effective learning for all students in your classroom.

—Debbie Metcalf
Interventionist, Pitt County Schools, Greenville, North Carolina
"Teacher-in-Residence," East Carolina University, Greenville, North Carolina

Sample Lesson Plans for Individuals With Intellectual Disabilities

1

Sample Lesson Plan 1.1 The Olympics—Past and Present

Area of Focus: Intellectual Disabilities

Subject: Social Studies

Grades: Elementary

Lesson Objective/s:	To research the history of the Olympics To compare and contrast Olympics of today to those in ancient Greece
Assessment/s:	Completed class Venn Diagram
State Standards Correlation:	(Social Studies) Describe how individuals, events, and ideas change over time
Materials/Resources:	Leveled books, websites, "Ode to Joy" by Beethoven, informational sheets with pictures of the Olympics past and present, gold medal replica or picture with athlete and medal, large Venn Diagram (may use hula hoops or plastic models) or Double Bubble Map (Thinking Maps), index cards, tape, toga (white sheet) with leaf crown for characterization
Preplanning Activities:	Set up music player, have vocabulary on cards (add pictures/symbols), prepare costumes, bookmark websites, print off informational sheets/pictures

Lesson Element	Procedure for Teacher and Materials	Potential Barriers for Learning: The student has challenges with . . .	UDL Multiple Means of . . . • Representation • Engagement • Expression
Lesson Opening	Questioning: • Do any of you know this song? • How many of you have watched the Olympics on TV? • What sports do you see at the Olympics today? • Does anyone know where the first Olympic Games were held? • Do you know what sports they had? Objective: Today we are going to learn more about the Olympics of today and long ago. Provide Advance Organizer: ✓ Read story ✓ List facts about today ✓ List facts with partner on index cards ✓ Place cards on Venn Diagram	Attention Motivation Recalling prior knowledge/ making connections Motivation Organization	Play part of the Olympic song, "Ode to Joy" by Beethoven. Hold up a gold medal or a picture of an Olympic athlete with a medal. Write objective on board. Use an advance organizer for step-by-step lists of tasks in lesson (or record it so it can be replayed as needed).

Phase	Activity	Need	Accommodation
Teacher Input	Show a short video clip of recent Olympics.	Language	Pre-teach and display vocabulary (ancient, athlete, chariot, compete, feast)—add pictures when possible.
	Tell, read, or show a story about the Olympics in ancient Greece.	Attention/memory	Add visuals to any stories when possible/dress up as an ancient Greek (in a toga) while telling the story.
	What did you see that was the same in ancient times and today? Model and place response on graphic organizer.	Comprehension	Stop frequently and ask students to talk about what they just heard with a partner.
Guided Practice	Generate list of what they learned about the Olympics in ancient Greece. (Teacher writes and posts on index cards.)	Language/cognition	Direct students to refer to vocabulary display (allow them to point or show).
	List a few student responses and model how to place them on a large graphic organizer for comparing/contrasting (Venn Diagram, double bubble Thinking Map).	Learned helplessness	Allow wait time.
			Offer frequent, positive feedback for participation, correct responses.
Independent Practice	Students will work in small groups to further research Olympics. Some will research the Olympics today and others in ancient times. They will write or draw facts they find on index cards or a poster.	Social interactions	Place students purposefully in cooperative learning groups (pair with positive models); Assign each student a role in his/her strength (a reader, a list maker, perhaps an illustrator).
		Difficulty attending	Allow computer research with read-aloud feature if needed (pre-select websites). Some pre-printed information sheets may also be helpful to have on hand.
		Remember rules, directions, transitions	Teacher circulates, asks guiding questions, and offers positive feedback for desired behaviors.
			Refer to rules and procedures posted in room.
Closure	Students come together and share what they learned by placing their index cards on a large Venn Diagram. What things are the same and which are different about the Olympics now and long ago? What did you learn?	Comprehension	Summarize what was learned today.
	Tomorrow we will learn about women's roles in the Olympics today and in ancient times.	Generalization	Set the stage for tomorrow.
			(Perhaps the student(s) know about Special Olympics and the teacher could talk informally with the student about that connection.)

A few students will point to their responses.

Some students will draw their responses.

All students will identify something that is the same and different about the Olympics now and then on the Venn Diagram.

Area of Focus: Intellectual Disabilities

Subject: Healthy Living

Grade: 9

Lesson Objective/s:	To identify a healthy eating plan for an athlete when home and away from home
Assessment/s:	Students' healthy eating plans
State Standards Correlation:	4.05 Demonstrate the ability to develop a healthful personal eating plan that incorporates food choices inside and outside of the home setting
Materials/Resources:	Some sports equipment, real examples of healthy food and junk food; video clips/bookmarked interactive websites on nutrition/sports nutrition; PowerPoint with projection, food pyramid chart/poster; Optional: Invite athletic trainer/athlete to visit
Preplanning Activities:	Prepare PowerPoint, scenarios for role play, blank organizer of food pyramid

Lesson Element	Procedure for Teacher and Materials	Potential Barriers for Learning: The student has challenges with . . .	UDL Multiple Means of . . . • Representation • Engagement • Expression
Lesson Opening	Questioning: How many of you participate in athletic events? Does what you eat make a difference in your performance? What can athletes do to improve their performance in the Olympics? Objective: Today we will come up with a healthy eating plan for an athlete.	Attention Motivation Activating prior learning	Tie into sports that you know the student participates in or enjoys watching. Have a real object from one or two of those sports to show. Hold up some healthy food and some junk food.
Teacher Input	Present information about fuel storage in humans and what fuels are used in exercise. Include energy, nutrients, and fluids in the presentation. Share what is recommended by sport nutritionists for most athletes. Show them wise and unwise food choices at home and outside of home.	Cognition/academic performance Transfer of information Comprehension	Invite an athlete or personal trainer to come talk to the class about healthy eating for exercise. Show a video clip or interactive website on sports nutrition. Use PowerPoint with visuals to convey information. Pause from time to time and have students summarize what they just learned with a partner. Show examples and non-examples of healthy foods (concrete or pictorial). Relate to poster of food pyramid.

4

Guided Practice	Have students talk about food choices they can make so they can perform their best physically.	Memory, generalization Modeling appropriate social skills	Have students role play food choices that can be made at home or outside of home after modeled by the teacher. Include props and some pre-planned scenarios.
Independent Practice	Students will use provided resources to expand their knowledge and show what they know about fuel for the body and healthy eating for athletes.	Outer-directedness	Students can choose researching sports nutrition through a webquest, construct a food pyramid for an athlete, or work with an interactive computer software program about nutrition.
		Independent work	Students may be allowed to work individually or with a peer.
		Learned helplessness	Teacher circulates, asks questions, and provides frequent positive feedback.
Closure	Students will share what they learned about what fuels help athletes and what they can eat both at home and outside of home to improve their performance.	Language	Students may present what they produced with a partner. One can explain verbally while the other points/shows.
		Transfer of information	Have students keep a food diary for a week and compare it to their healthy eating plans. Provide a template and post it to the class website.

Some students will research sports nutrition websites and design an eating plan for an athlete in a specific sport.

Most students will construct a food pyramid that highlights a healthy eating plan for most athletes.

All students will identify a healthy eating plan for an athlete.

Sample Lesson Plans for Individuals With Learning Disabilities

2

Sample Lesson Plan 2.1   All-Star Athletes

Area of Focus: Learning Disabilities

Subject: English Language Arts

Grade: 3

Lesson Objective/s:	To research an Olympic athlete and produce an illustrated report
Assessment/s:	Completed reports
State Standards Correlation:	3.06 Conduct research for assigned and self-selected projects (with assistance) from a variety of sources (e.g., print and non-print texts, artifacts, people, libraries, databases, computer networks); 4.10 Explore technology as a tool to create a written product
Materials/Resources:	Posters/pictures of athletes students may know or identify with, document projector, Circle Map (Thinking Maps), MP3 players or iPods (or lower-tech recording device), Read & Write GOLD software, spell checker/dictionary, document projector or overhead, computer access for students, index cards, graphic organizers
Preplanning Activities:	Prepare direction cards, sample graphic organizer and storyboard, record directions on MP3 player or iPod, reserve computer lab if necessary

Lesson Element	Procedure for Teacher and Materials	Potential Barriers for Learning: The student has challenges with . . .	UDL Multiple Means of . . . • Representation • Engagement • Expression
Lesson Opening	Do you have a favorite Olympic athlete? What is your favorite sport to watch? Objective: Today you will have the opportunity to research an Olympic athlete using the computer. We will put these reports together to make a class book! Advance Organizer: ✓ Research athlete ✓ Use a graphic organizer to brainstorm ideas ✓ Write two paragraphs ✓ Edit with teacher ✓ Word process ✓ Illustrate with paint program	Attention Motivation Focus Organization	Have pictures or a poster at hand with athletes they are likely to know. Be enthusiastic! Write objective on board. Post and refer to advance organizer.

Teacher Input	Read a sample report on an Olympic athlete. Show an illustration with it.	Organization	Have the report you are reading projected using a document projector or on the overhead.
	Explain the research project steps. Demonstrate the graphic organizer.	Reading	Use a read-aloud application during computer research or work with a buddy who can assist with reading.
			Graphic organizer for brainstorming.
	Have students choose different athletes from a list.	Metacognition	
	Provide lists of websites and have them bookmarked on the computer.	Memory	Have 4 x 6 index cards available so students can write each paragraph on a separate card.
			Record directions/task steps on an MP3 player for easy repetition.
			Have choices and direction steps for paint program on a card by the computer.
		Spelling	Have spelling checkers available for writing/editing.
Guided Practice	Have websites bookmarked for each athlete. Have students open their links. Have students take notes on their graphic organizer.	Processing	Have teacher computer projected onto large screen or have document projector nearby to model using the graphic organizer.
	Show students how they can add a Web graphic, clip art, or original art using a paint program.		Model adding visuals to reports when they have finished constructing graphic organizer.
Independent Practice	Students research, brainstorm, create a rough draft, edit, word process, and illustrate their research reports.	Writing	Allow student to make a storyboard about his/her athlete with pictures and/or words.
		Learned helplessness	Allow student to record information on an iPod or other recorder. Recording may be referred to when word processing.
		Attention	Circulate among students, ask questions, provide frequent positive feedback.
			Allow students to sit on a ball chair or use a fidget.
Closure	Students share reports and compile to make a class book.	Language	Allow student to rehearse presenting report with teacher or another student first.

Some students will construct pictorial storyboards with limited support.

Most students will complete organizers or storyboards independently using words and pictures.

All students will share a report and contribute to class book.

Sample Lesson Plan 2.2   Olympic Newscasts

Area of Focus: Learning Disabilities

Subject: English Language Arts

Grades: Secondary

Lesson Objective/s:	Students will research different events featured in the Winter (or Summer) Olympics and produce newscasts about them
Assessment/s:	Completed graphic organizer with sharing of one cool fact about their sport
State Standards Correlation:	2.01 Demonstrate the ability to read, listen to, and view a variety of increasingly complex print and non-print informational texts appropriate to grade level and course literary focus, by summarizing key events and/or points from text, and 6.01 Demonstrate an understanding of conventional written and spoken expression
Materials/Resources:	Video clip with closed caption/articles on Olympic sports, Read & Write GOLD or other text to speech software, index cards, electronic whiteboard or overhead
Preplanning Activities:	Laminate organizers and gather markers/erasers, prepare list of possible athlete choices with labels/pictures; informational cards for different sports/bookmarked websites and/or related information sheets; Reserve computer lab if needed; Divide up tasks with co-teacher

Lesson Element	Procedure for Teacher and Materials	Potential Barriers for Learning: The student has challenges with . . .	UDL Multiple Means of . . . • **Representation** • **Engagement** • **Expression**
Lesson Opening	Ask students what they know about the Winter Olympics. What do they know about sports such as luge, snowboarding, skeleton, curling? Do they know who the athletes are from their country? Objective: Today you will be researchers/reporters and begin prepare newscasts about some of these different winter sport events. Advance Organizer: ✓ Watch news clip ✓ Read article ✓ View demonstration with graphic organizer ✓ Research sport for your newscast ✓ Complete graphic organizer ✓ Find and share one cool fact about your sport	Focus, attention Motivation Organization Self-monitoring	Ask questions. Name different sports and athletes from their country and have students raise hands if they are familiar or not with these sports/athletes. Tally their responses on board. Keep a brisk pace. Write objective on board. Have organizer posted in room for easy reference or student copy on desk or recorded at desk if needed.

	Activities	Difficulties	Accommodations
Teacher Input	Open with a news clip on one winter sport students are likely familiar with or interested in (such as snowboarding).	Decoding text	Use video streaming, internet news source with projection (optional: apply closed captions to help with reading fluency).
	Provide an informational article on this same sport and view it together.		Provide an online or scanned article that can be projected as it is read aloud by teacher or other audio.
	Pass out laminated organizers. Ask students to see if they can identify the 5 W and H questions that help reporters write newscasts while you view the article with them.	Comprehending text	Put what was just viewed with a partner (Think-Pair-Share).
	Name an athlete from your country who has or will compete in this sport (under Who).	Metacognition / Organization	Introduce graphic organizer for pre-writing/thinking.
	Highlight one cool fact about the sport.	Motivation	Students choose a sport they are interested in.
		Memory / Language retrieval difficulties / May not have background knowledge	Have a list of possible athlete choices (with pictures if possible) to show.
Guided Practice	Review and complete that same graphic organizer with them (Who, What, Where, When, Why, How) about this sport together.	Difficulty understanding directions or what is heard	Teacher has model on overhead or electronic whiteboard and fills in as students respond.
	Find one cool fact about it.	Strategic applications	Highlight places the information was found in the article as the organizer is completed (electronic highlighting feature or with colored pen on overhead).
Independent Practice	Have students research another Winter Olympic sport.	Learned helplessness	Have sports listed on cards with web links and other available resources noted.
	Complete organizer.	Memory	
	Find one cool fact about it.	Reading	Apply text to speech computer application or pair with student who can assist with reading.
Closure	Students share one cool fact about their sport with the whole group.	Language / Memory	Allow students to rehearse responses with teacher or peer during independent practice. Have fact written or drawn on index card.
	"Tomorrow we will use our organizers to write a newscast about your sport. You will work with a partner. See if you can find out any more information about your sport before I see you again."	Keeping a positive attitude	Tell students what a great job they did on this today and how much you enjoyed learning about their athletes!
		Making connections	Talk about how this lesson will continue; ask students to connect to environment outside of school—write in homework planner; involve parents.

Some students will need extra support from peers or adults to scaffold assignment.

Most students will complete these tasks with extra support for decoding only after receiving modeling and direct instruction.

All students will complete a graphic organizer about an Olympic sport and share a cool fact.

Sample Lesson Plans for Individuals With Attention Deficit Hyperactivity Disorder

3

3.1   Elementary: Olympic Medals

3.2   Secondary: Using Sports to Explain Statistical Concepts

Area of Focus: ADHD

Subject: Mathematics

Grade: 3

Lesson Objective/s:	To make a bar graph using data
Assessment/s:	Students will identify steps in creating a bar graph
State Standards Correlation:	4.01 Collect, organize, analyze, and display data to solve problems
Materials/Resources:	Large paper, markers, post-its; overhead or other projection; computers
Preplanning Activities:	Vocabulary with visuals, advance organizer posted in room; Co-teacher reviews key vocabulary prior to lesson with small group; Prepare and hole punch index cards with graphing steps for student strategy "rings"; Draw grid lines on large paper (use colored tape for lines); Put country names in bag

Lesson Element	Procedure for Teacher and Materials	Potential Barriers for Learning: The student has challenges with . . .	UDL Multiple Means of . . . • Representation • Engagement • Expression
Lesson Opening	"It's time to begin math. What countries are participating in the Olympics?" Objective: Today we will make a bar graph to see how different countries are doing in the Olympic medal count. Advance Organizer: ✓ Make a bar graph using 6 steps ✓ Graph medals for the USA ✓ Graph medals for your country ✓ Compare and contrast data	Focusing Motivation Making connections Reasoning Organization	Have a visual or auditory signal to begin the class (a bell, clapping pattern that students repeat, for example). Be sure students know what they are learning and why. Review classroom rules and expectations. Provide advance organizer on chart and/or individual cards/paper as needed. Add visual/symbols as needed.
Teacher Input	Class, there are 6 steps in making a bar graph: 1. *First,* name your graph. 2. *Next,* draw the vertical and horizontal axes on your graph. 3. *Then,* label the horizontal axis (Countries). 4. Label the vertical axes (# of medals) here. 5. Decide on the scale of your graph. 6. Draw a bar to show total for each column.	Focusing on what is important Following directions Organization	Review vocabulary words and have them posted in room with visual examples (vertical axis, horizontal axis, scale, range) of previously learned words. Demonstration teaching. Students have individual whiteboards or laminated organizers at their desk to model teacher (some whiteboards have imprinted graph lines). Number and use transitional words while progressing through steps. Have a poster or other visual with steps of making a bar graph on display.
Guided Practice	Review the 6 steps in making a bar graph. Use post-it notes to represent every 5 medals on the large graph. Post-its can be cut to show smaller numerical representations.	Executive functioning Staying focused Memory	Backward chaining. Present steps visually on poster, overhead, or other projection. Chorally read/say all steps. Cover up last step. Say all steps. Cover last 2 steps. Repeat process until all steps are covered up.

		Focus Memory Needs movement	Provide students with card that lists the steps in making a bar graph or have steps recorded on a switch or MP3 player for auditory access. Pass out 6 post-its to students and have them come place them on the bar graph as data is compiled.
Independent Practice	Students draw a country name out of a bag and find their partner. Students research newspapers, media to find the number of medals won each day by that country. Students determine number of medals for that country and record on post-its. Students may draw another country name from the bag if done early. Extensions: Have students create an electronic graph by the types of medals won (gold, silver, bronze). Give 5-minute transition cue.	Paying attention Blurting out Following rules Hyperactivity/fidgeting Difficulty with unstructured time Focusing Self-confidence Student needs extra challenge Transitions/Planning	Students will work in pairs. (Teacher may pre-determine partners.) One person from the team will draw country name from the bag. Refer to class rules that are posted in room as needed. Compliment positive behaviors. Use established contingency management system if needed. Allow students to sit on ball chairs, to or stand up as long as they are on task. Allow them to hold a fidget as long as they follow the rules. Provide extra practice. Teacher circulates, asks questions, provides specific feedback and praise. Check to see that students have correct # of post-its to add to class graph. Complete extension; graph data using computer spreadsheet. Statement of time remaining to finish.
Closure	"Let's come back together and add your findings to our bar graph." Students raise hands to answer teacher-generated questions about the graph. Review number of steps in making a bar graph. "Before you line up, place your index cards on your strategy ring to refer to when you do your homework."	Transition Movement Taking turns Blurting out Memory Processing Organization Transition	Use same visual or auditory signal to return to large group. Students bring up post-its for their country to add to graph. Teacher or student helper can write in name of country. Everyone counts. State behavioral expectation before question. Numbering and naming bar graph steps together out loud. Telling what they learned today. Cue upcoming transition and tend to notebook organization.

A few students will complete a graph comparing gold, silver, and bronze medals awarded on an Excel spreadsheet.

Some students will find gold medal data on more than one country.

All students will identify the steps in making a bar graph to display data.

Sample Lesson Plan 3.2 Using Sports to Explain Statistical Concepts

Area of Focus: ADHD

Subject: Algebra

Grades: Secondary

Lesson Objective/s:	Calculate and interpret the range, quartiles, and inter-quartile range of a set of data
Assessment/s:	Individual data results compiled by students and their explanations (teacher recording)
State Standards Correlation:	Standards Correlation: 4.01 Collect, organize, analyze, and display data to solve problems
Materials/Resources:	Cotton balls, post-its to mark landing, individual dry erase board with markers, index cards
Preplanning Activities:	Prepare new vocabulary words and add symbolic representation/example/visualization (if there is a co-teacher, pre-teach vocabulary before class begins); Prepare class advance organizer and some individual ones. Have any self-monitoring sheets ready for students who need them

Lesson Element	Procedure for Teacher and Materials	Potential Barriers for Learning: The student has challenges with . . .	UDL Multiple Means of . . . • **Representation** • **Engagement** • **Expression**

Lesson Opening	Teacher throws several cotton balls one at a time in one direction and then measures the distance of each.
	
	Objective: Today we are going to look at how to separate and organize a set of data we collect on a variable.
	
	You will all be part of our data collection. Let's review our rules and procedures.
	
	Advance Organizer:
	
	  ✓ Review vocabulary
	  ✓ Draw x axis
	  ✓ Generate data
	  ✓ Collect data
	  ✓ Arrange data on x axis
	
	Analyze data.
		Attending
		Focusing
		
		Motivation
			Use novelty.
			
			Post objective and advance organizer in room. Review both and refer to throughout lesson as needed (verbally or by pointing). Have individual copies available as needed.

		Vocabulary/terminology and their definitions	Review and introduce new vocabulary: variable, variation, range, quartile, inter-quartile range, outliers.
Teacher Input	Introduce terminology and demonstrate • Measures of variation • Range • Upper and lower quartiles • Inter-quartile range • Outliers Explain/show the differences between quartiles.		Place new words on Word Wall (and on index cards to add to individual student vocabulary rings). Demonstrate on chart how data is arranged and grouped while thinking aloud. Then demonstrate with cotton balls while thinking aloud.
Guided Practice	Teacher leads students • Everyone draws x axis to mark their data • Talk about how a scale will be established • Students generate data by throwing cotton balls and measuring • Arrange collected data on x axis • All students analyze same data and draw conclusions	Focusing Attending to new material Staying in seat, sitting still Self-confidence	Students have individual whiteboards and model teacher demonstration. Use cotton balls that are colored to represent different students (or teams of students) who are demonstrating this. One student at a time stands to throw, others wait on "sidelines." Acknowledge positive behavior.
Independent Practice	The teacher introduces a Winter Olympics event—the large hill downhill ski jump, for example. Teacher provides jump distance data. Students independently analyze data.	Attending to task Working independently	Use colored adhesive dots for marking data. Student may use self-monitoring checklist if needed. May work with partner or on computer with program that scaffolds this same instruction. Teacher circulates, questions, provides needed cues/prompts/feedback.
Closure	Look at the results of the data shown by range, upper and lower quartiles, inter-quartile range, ranges, and outliers. Ask students what this display of data shows. "Tomorrow we will add another variable. We will look at the distance of the ski jumps along with the heights."	Seeing cause/effect Drawing conclusions Staying on task Self-confidence Transitioning to new learning	Sharing data results. Asking questions. Thinking aloud. Praising students for their attempts. Previewing next lesson.

Some students will identify outliers using a given formula.

Most students will identify and separate the numbers of data points into quartiles whether they are odd or even numbers.

All students will identify and separate an even number of data points into quartiles. They will put them in numerical sequence to make a table.

17

Sample Lesson Plans for Individuals With Emotional or Behavioral Disorders

4

4.1   Elementary: Olympic Haiku Poetry

4.2   Secondary: Heroes

Area of Focus: Emotional or Behavioral Disorders

Subject: Writing Poetry

Grade: 3

Lesson Objective/s:	To identify the components of a haiku; To construct a haiku poem
Assessment/s:	Completed haiku with rubric
State Standards Correlation:	ELA 4.07 Compose a variety of fiction, non-fiction, poetry, and drama selections using self-selected topics and forms
Materials/Resources:	Collect haiku poetry examples
Preplanning Activities:	Prepare haikus to use as examples, prepare graphic organizer for haiku writing; Check classroom orderliness, lighting (natural preferred), temperature of classroom; Have a plan within the classroom or with another teacher or staff member if "time away" is needed for a student; Have any needed behavior cards ready

Lesson Element	Procedure for Teacher and Materials	Potential Barriers for Learning: The student has challenges with . . .	UDL Multiple Means of . . . • Representation • Engagement • Expression
Lesson Opening	Read an example haiku poem: A snowy village A skater goes swiftly by Applause! People cheer What did you think of when you heard the poem? Does it make you feel like you are at the Olympics? Objective: Today we try writing this kind of poem to help express how we feel about the Olympics or other events. Advance Organizer: ✓ Choose picture ✓ Think of words ✓ Write 3 syllables for each word ✓ Write haiku ✓ Illustrate	Following rules Handling unstructured time Student is disruptive Motivation Student lacks self-confidence Student has difficulty internalizing/generalizing rules Organization Scheduling	Post rules with consequences and schedule in prominent place in classroom. Be sure student is sitting in easy visual access to teacher. Frequent questioning. Student seated near teacher. State objective and purpose for lesson. Praise student attempts to participate. Review class schedule/procedures. Review advance organizer.
Teacher Input	Who can remember what kinds of poetry we have written so far? The kind of poetry we are working with today is called haiku. It originally came from Japan. A haiku has a 5-7-5 syllable structure. (Count syllables on the sample poem in opening.) These poems are usually about nature. They can help you put words with a feeling you have about nature or another subject. Have students think of nature words and count the syllables.	Activating prior knowledge May lack vocabulary/language Students are off task or disruptive Memory Students need routine	Review prior knowledge and vocabulary learned to date (shape poem, cinquain, limerick, and add haiku). Refer back to rules as needed (visually, physically, or verbally). Present new information in small steps. Refer back to advance organizer to cue student into steps they are on in the lesson. Provide a more explicit assignment checklist if needed.

Phase	Activity	Student need / behavior	Accommodations
		Student is aggressive/disruptive	Ask questions frequently to help student engage. Provide positive feedback.
		Student is off task	Allow fidget or alternate seating if needed and if rules for that privilege are understood ahead of time.
Guided Practice	Show students a picture of an Olympic scene (summer or winter) or other athletic event. Ask students to brainstorm words about the picture. Write/draw them in a large circle map. Talk aloud about ideas they have about the picture. Go back and write the syllable count for each brainstormed word in parentheses after each word. Using a haiku graphic organizer, write a class haiku using these words. Illustrate it.	Attending Interacting Comprehending Vocabulary Structure, organization	Show pictures, ask questions, talk together about ideas. Model on chart, overhead of poem. Provide content enhancements (such as graphic organizers).
Independent Practice	Provide students with different pictures that feature athletes. Have them choose one and brainstorm words about it. Illustrate.	Student needs feeling of some control/power Student has difficulty working independently Attention Self-confidence Student needs quiet space to work	Allow some opportunities for choice. Provide extra practice during this time if needed. Review and discuss schedule, procedures, and rules with student. Provide interactive computer program to create haiku. Provide behavioral/self-monitoring checklists/charts for students as needed. Circulate and provide positive and corrective feedback. Praise students who are working. Allow student to work at study carrel.
Closure	Share haikus with class. Display in hallway.	Transitioning back to group and then to next activity Self-confidence Task completion	Have a verbal, visual, or physical cue (blinking lights, gesture, ring bell, for example) for transitions. Praise students for their efforts. Display completed haikus. Submit some to newspaper for publishing.

Some students will research the history of haiku poetry and compare and contrast Japanese and American haiku poetry.

Most students will create a haiku poem and express two or more characteristics of haiku poetry.

All students will create a haiku poem and tell or show one characteristic of haiku poetry.

21

Sample Lesson Plan 4.2 Heroes

Area of Focus: SED

Subject: ELA/Healthful Living

Grades: Middle School

Lesson Objective/s:	To identify and communicate the character traits of heroes
Assessment/s:	Project rubric
State Standards Correlation:	ELA: 2.01 Respond to informational materials that are read, heard, and/or viewed; 6.01 Model an understanding of conventional written and spoken expression; Healthful Living 1.04 Recognize that failure is a part of learning and growing and demonstrate the ability to cope with failure appropriately
Materials/Resources:	Collect information about Olympic and other popular cultural values from print resources and websites; samples of product choices. Find a video clip of one of Michael Phelps's Olympic medal swimming events
Preplanning Activities:	Have all individual behavior card systems in place. Have centers ready for writing and art; Have pictures of athlete choices ready for lesson body; Prepare samples of writing report, song/rap, and medal. Prepare rubrics for each activity

Lesson Element	Procedure for Teacher and Materials	Potential Barriers for Learning: The student has challenges with . . .	UDL Multiple Means of . . . • Representation • Engagement • Expression
Lesson Opening	What does it mean to be a hero? (List responses on board and save) Objective: Today we will explore some characteristics of people who make a difference. Advance Organizer ✓ Define hero ✓ Watch video clip ✓ Discussion ✓ Choose a hero ✓ Research report or create medal ✓ Check with rubric ✓ Share with class	Motivation Making connections to prior learning Following rules Changes in schedule Self-monitoring	Play a hero song such "Hero" by Mariah Carey or "Looking Out for a Hero" (from Footloose) while transitioning to lesson. We have been talking about people who have made a difference. Have objective(s) posted on board/chart. Go over rules and behavior expectations that are pertinent to the lesson. (Full set of classroom rules visible in room) Notify students of any changes to schedule in advance. Post advance organizer and provide an individual assignment checklist as needed.

Teacher Input	Do you know any heroes? Many of us have been watching the Olympic Games. These Games show us the importance of values such as friendship, fair play, commitment, perseverance, and respect. Show a video clip of an Olympic athlete like Michael Phelps who has overcome an obstacle and provide part of the personal story. What characteristics do you see (team player, kind, truthful, respectful)? Tell them that Michael has ADHD and he didn't always have the easiest time in school (students sometimes picked on him because of how he looked and called him "Gomer") yet he stayed friendly and worked hard to pour his extra energy into swimming. Even heroes sometimes make unwise choices (provide real-life example). Show predesigned medal for Michael Phelps. Talk about other kinds of heroes: firefighters, media stars, soldiers, other sports figures. Questions: Do all heroes make lots of money? Can heroes be people you know? Can you be a hero?	Being interested Motivation Empathy Bullying, teasing Making good choices Novelty/motivation Comprehension Focusing	Tap into what they find relevant. Film clips can show faces/emotions while telling the story; the visual images can increase engagement. Offer a real-life example. Give examples and non-examples. Provide samples to preview work. Check for understanding. Make connections. Ask questions. Encourage full participation.
Guided Practice	As you look through these pictures with me, your task is to find someone you view as a hero. Students will prepare a report, song/rap or create a medal that describes the hero selected. Then find at least 2 examples of values that describe what makes this person a hero. Explain the directions and give an example and rubric for each choice. (For the medal example, a medal for Michael Phelps can be shown. It might include his name, his picture, and a swimsuit. There is a heart because he is kind and a drawing of him with other swimmers because he is a team player.) Review the graphic organizers they can use for their products. You have a green card and a red card on your desk. Raise the red card if you need help.	Help with structure Making connections Need for control Following instructions Need for structure	Show some Olympic heroes you think they might enjoy researching. Have hard or electronic copies of these athletes. Have students choose and write their choices on the board/overhead. If students can't find an Olympic athlete they want to research, allow an appropriate hero choice from another sport or category of interest. Allow student to choose between activities for expression: writing a report, or writing a song/rap, or creating a medal. Have a sample of completed project choices (song lyrics from your lesson opening, report, medal sample). The short story you tell about the teacher-highlighted athlete can be the written report. Provide sample rubrics for each activity choice that they can also use to review steps and requirements. Provide flow maps for those writing reports or songs/raps. Provide a graphic organizer of a medal for brainstorming (use it as a semantic web or circle map from Thinking Maps).

		Paper and pencil tasks	Allow students to create their reports or songs/raps on portable keyboards, computers, or record them as audio files.
		Staying motivated	Allow students to add instruments to their songs/raps (computerized or real). Provide art materials and templates for medal construction. Students may draw, print value words, use art materials to design symbols.
		Writing, motivation, or interest	Teacher circulates and provides frequent, positive, specific corrective feedback.
		Staying on task Understanding Asking for help Being disruptive	Have a non-verbal system in place for students who have questions or need help.
Independent Practice	Extension: Create a webquest that highlights different Olympians who have inspirational heroic stories. Interview people in your school or community that you view as heroes.	Needs more challenge	Computers with Inspiration software and internet access for webquest. If interviewing, they can prepare questions and arrange for interviews times with these people.
Closure	Share products. Let's look back at our list. Are there any other characteristics of heroes to add? What are some examples of heroes in our community? How can you be a hero? Thank you for working so hard today and sharing what you learned. Tomorrow we will use our products to make a newscast about heroes.	Being respectful, sharing Need for routine Making connections Transferring Social skills Connected learning Individual behavior contingency management systems or contracts	Review rules that apply for being respectful, listening. Go back to chart and write additions. Questioning, reinforcing. Continually modeling appropriate social skills. Check any behavior cards.

Some students will create a webquest that highlights different Olympians who have inspirational heroic stories. They will write an introduction to the webquest that identifies 4 or more similar characteristics, including two or more values, of these heroes.

Most students will give 3 or more characteristics, including one or more values, of their hero in their product.

All students will produce either a report, song, or medal that identifies 2 characteristics, including at least one value, of their hero.

Sample Lesson Plans for Individuals With Autism Spectrum Disorders

5

5.1 Elementary: Friends Around the World

5.2 Secondary: Sportsmanship and Determination

Sample Lesson Plan 5.1 Friends Around the World

Area of Focus: Autism Spectrum Disorders

Subject: Music/English Language Arts

Grades: Elementary

Lesson Objective/s:	To identify characteristics of Olympic friendships through music
Assessment/s:	Student performance with rubric
State Standards Correlation:	2.05 Play independent instrumental parts while others sing and/or play rhythmic, melodic, or harmonic parts; 2.07 Play music representing diverse styles, genres, and cultures; English Language Arts 4.01 Read aloud grade-appropriate text with fluency, comprehension, and expression demonstrating an awareness of volume and pace
Materials/Resources:	Students will need access to hear and play music (computers, MP3 players, other audio devices). Gather triangles, bells, claves, maracas, drums of different sizes/types
Preplanning Activities:	Prepare/gather examples and non-examples of friendship on cards from social skills kits, internet, books (or use role play/puppets); Find an inspirational Olympic friendship story students can likely relate to; Gather songs that relate to friendship with lyrics that can be projected; Minimize visual and auditory distractions as much as possible

Lesson Element	Procedure for Teacher and Materials	Potential Barriers for Learning: The student has challenges with . . .	UDL Multiple Means of . . . • **Representation** • **Engagement** • **Expression**
Lesson Opening	Remember yesterday we talked about music and emotions. Do you feel the emotions in this music? What are they?	Focusing/transitioning	Play a friendship song (such as James Taylor's "You've Got a Friend").
	Objective: Today we are going to celebrate the value of friendships that are made through the Olympics through music	Motivation Making a personal connection	Refer to emotions poster displayed in room (faces with different emotions). Be positive!
	Review rules and visual schedule.	Following rules/procedures Disruptive behavior	Review rules and visual schedule posted in class. Implement student's individual behavior plan.
Teacher Input	Questioning: What is a friend? How do people make new friends? How can someone be a better friend? If someone is not a friend, what does that look like?	Attention Concentration Language Abstract thinking	Write any ideas on board/Add visuals. Offer some examples of things you can say to or ask friends. Examples and non-examples on picture cards that student can point to, or hold up (or role play with another adult in the room).
	The Olympics brings people from all over the world together. Many friendships are made between strangers. Friendships are an important value of the Olympics. Share an Olympic friendship story, if possible.	Connecting to real life	Show a short video clip or illustrated book/projected digital book of an Olympic friendship story. It could be a Special Olympic friendship story depending upon student need/interests.

Phase	Description	Need	Accommodations
	When people work together toward a goal, friendships can develop. They can be working on the same sports team, on a news broadcasting team, or a team of volunteers who help make the events happen. When have you worked with other people toward a common goal?		Refer to pictures that show friends working together. Have students talk briefly with a partner (Think-Pair-Share). Pair any non-verbal students with verbal students. Share in large group.
Guided Practice	What songs or music make you think about friendship? Let's listen to a few songs and see if we can identify characteristics that make them effective in conveying this emotion. Play parts of songs such as "A Whole New World," "Lean on Me," "With a Little Help From My Friends," "It's a Small World," "I'll Be There," "Wind Beneath My Wings." List student responses on board or chart. Provide students with choices of friendship songs with lyrics and have them choose one to learn as a group and add musical instruments and movement.	Attention Language Non-verbal student Visual representation Needs structure Understanding and remembering directions	Play parts of different songs about friendship. Project the lyrics and have students follow along as they sing. Stop and ask students what they can name, feel, or show about friendship (non-verbal students may point to face on emotion chart or other picture/visual that was shared earlier). Add words/symbols to listed words whenever possible. Refer back to rules, schedule as needed. Break down task with students as you work together. Use key words in directions. Add musical instruments one at a time. Add gestures gradually and provide multiple practice opportunities.
Independent Practice	Extension: Some students could create their own song or social story about friendship and add instruments, other sound, and/or movement.	Needs easier or more difficult text Has difficulty working independently	Provide lyrics, poems on different reading levels. Student can work with a partner or coach depending upon need.
Closure	Give students response cards and say or act out a few examples/non-examples from lesson body. Talk about what they learned about friendship and music. Relate back to why friendship is an important value of the Olympics.	Using language Making connections Transition	Students each have yes/no response cards. They hold up card that indicates they can distinguish between examples and non-examples of friendship characteristics. Prepare students for transition. Refer to visual schedule. Play a closing song as students transition to next class or activity.

Some students will create a song or social story about friendship.

Most students will distinguish correctly between examples and non-examples of friendship characteristics.

All students will informally perform a song about friendship adding rhythmic parts with instruments and/or movement to the music.

Sample Lesson Plan 5.2 Sportsmanship and Determination

Area of Focus: Autism Spectrum Disorder

Subject: English Language Arts/Healthful Living

Grades: Middle School/Secondary General Curriculum

Lesson Objective/s:	To create a social story based on sportsmanship or the determination needed to be an Olympian
Assessment/s:	Group or individual social story with rubric
State Standards Correlation:	ELA 1.02 Respond reflectively to a variety of expressive texts in a way that offers an audience an understanding of the student's personal reaction to the text; Healthful Living 10.01 Demonstrate respect for individual differences in physical activity settings utilizing character education and sportsmanship
Materials/Resources:	http://www.polyxo.com/socialstories/introduction.html (provides examples and how to write them); http://www.thegraycenter.org/ (more examples, template); Writing Symbols, Boardmaker, computer, storyboards/flow maps
Preplanning Activities:	Find a video clip or book of an athlete who has an inspiring story of sportsmanship or determination. Provide an advance organizer, schedule, and rules. Prepare any individual behavior monitoring cards/charts. Collect pictures/clip art in folder on computer (or hard copies) to use in guided practice when creating storyboard

Lesson Element	Procedure for Teacher and Materials	Potential Barriers for Learning: The student has challenges with . . .	UDL Multiple Means of . . . • Representation • Engagement • Expression
Lesson Opening	What do you say when your team make a mistake or loses? What can you tell yourself when you get frustrated because things all seem to go wrong? Objective: Today we are going to work on stories that tell about people who have to work very hard to reach their goals. We will use computers. Advance Organizer: ✓ Watch Olympic story ✓ Create storyboard or flow map with group ✓ Research another Olympic athlete ✓ Create flow map on your own ✓ Share with class	Activating prior knowledge Language Motivation Scheduling Disruptive behavior	Refer to a team student(s) is/are on. Use language student is familiar with. Be as clear as possible. Be positive and enthusiastic. Post visual structure for reference including advance organizer/Add visuals as needed. Have rules/procedures posted; review as necessary. Students have individual behavior monitoring cards as needed.

Teacher Input	Olympic athletes have to work very hard. They sometimes get frustrated. Here is a story about an athlete who may have wanted to give up but didn't and met his/her goal. What did you learn from this story?	Receptive/expressive language Difficulty with decoding and/or comprehension	Review key vocabulary: frustration, sportsmanship, determination (add visualizations/symbols). Use language student can relate to in personal life. Show video of inspirational Olympic athlete. Summarize what was seen and heard. Allow wait time for oral responses.
Guided Practice	Teacher shows pictures/clip art that portray this same sports player who faced a problem and solves it with sportsmanship or determination. Using a large storyboard or flow map for sequencing (Thinking Maps), have students decide where to place pictures. Ask them for appropriate captions.	Making real life/literal connections Cause/effect Breaking down tasks Organizing Speaking/writing	Relate story to something that student can identify with. Modeling. Students work with the teacher in developing a class social story. This can be done on paper, or PowerPoint. Students help choose clip art or draw pictures to create the group storyboard.
Independent Practice	Research an Olympic athlete who has shown outstanding sportsmanship or determination. Pre-write using a flow map. Use it to write a 3-paragraph narrative. Extension: Some students may want to write social stories for other students with special needs in the school on one of these topics to house in the school media center.	Generating writing ideas Organizing Writing Working independently Managing unstructured time	Provide graphic organizers for independent writing (flow maps). Have students use pictures first and then provide captions. Provide captions for script. Provide different writing tools or word processing for students to write about each picture in the group story. Non-verbal students can write using a program such as *Writing Symbols* or add pictures using *Boardmaker*. May work with peer or teacher. Reference rules/procedures/behavior cards.
Closure	Share narratives/social stories with class. What did you learn about sportsmanship and determination?	Language Interactions with others Making connections	Share social story with a peer. Express what was learned.

Some students will add writing symbols to the group social story.

Most students will add text or captions using pencil/pen or word processing.

All students will create a visual social story.

Sample Lesson Plans for Individuals With Speech and Language Disorders

6

6.1   Elementary: We Are the Champions

6.2   Secondary: RAP a Paragraph

Area of Focus: Speech/Language

Subject: English Language Arts

Grades: Elementary (2)

Lesson Objective/s:	To read or sing a song/poem about the Olympics
Assessment/s:	Performance recording with rubric
State Standards Correlation:	4.03 Read aloud with fluency and expression any text appropriate for early independent readers
Materials/Resources:	Winter Olympic Code, song, or poem for choral reading (find or write an age-appropriate song/poem/reading that has a lot of repetition, some different parts, and a chorus. A music teacher is often quite willing to help with this.), technology for recording/playing music; Identify Target Vocabulary from material and review/display
Preplanning Activities:	Collect play, song/music, props; Have scripts/lyrics in a format that can be projected visually. Have individual copies available. Pre-recorded copies that students can listen to can also help some learners. Arrange with music teacher to borrow hand-held instruments or perhaps to accompany final product

Lesson Element	Procedure for Teacher and Materials	Potential Barriers for Learning: The student has challenges with . . .	UDL Multiple Means of . . . • **Representation** • **Engagement** • **Expression**
Lesson Opening	Play a short part of the opening Olympic theme song composed by John Williams or other sports-related songs students will relate to (such as "Rocky" or "We Are the Champions").	Motivation/attention Activating prior knowledge	Play familiar music related to the theme.
		Auditory processing	Provide simple, clear directions.
	Objective: Class, today you will have the opportunity to be part of an Olympic team. We will use a choral reading and song to tell our story.	Following directions	Provide advance organizer.
Teacher Input	Teacher will display reading/song.	Following along Auditory processing	Have song/poem projected on large screen; perhaps student could track words for class with a pointer.
	Teacher models reading all or part of the reading/song, depending upon length.	Limited vocabulary	Have key vocabulary on cards with visual representation. Review and display in room.
	Teacher assigns parts.	Processing	Chunk the reading or song into manageable parts for rehearsal.
	Teacher demonstrates how props/instruments and/or movement can be added to make it more interesting.	Producing sounds Stuttering	Have student sing/speak with chorus or pair with another sports figure for responses.
		Reluctant to participate	Offer choice for parts.
			Be positive!
			Add some props and/or a musical instrument that students can play to participate.
			Student may use a switch that has his/her part prerecorded.
		Non-verbal	Add movement, sign language.

32

Guided Practice	Assign parts such as skaters, skiers, hockey players, gold medalists. Everyone reads chorus. Everyone practices.	Difficulty reading Memory Language processing	Level different parts of text/poem and assign accordingly so that all can read at their level. Practice chorus multiple times. Keep visual with words projected in room or on a chart. Some students may benefit from individual copies.
Independent Practice	Students work in small groups to practice their parts. Extension: A new Olympic song is needed for the 2012 games. Create a song, reading, or poem for it.	Fear of rejection Confidence	Pair/group students carefully. Spend extra time modeling/practicing with students to use language, speech, gestures. Build in extra opportunities to rehearse responses. Circulate, ask questions, provide feedback and positive reinforcement.
Closure	Perform the reading/song and record it. Ask students what they learned.	Fluent speech Stuttering	Put it to music in a song.

Some students will create words to a song, reading, or poem for the next Olympic games.

Most students will successfully produce the words needed to express their parts in the reading/song at appropriate times.

All students will participate successfully in the choral reading or song (verbally or non-verbally).

Sample Lesson Plan 6.2   RAP a Paragraph

Area of Focus: Speech/Language

Subject: Getting the Main Idea/Comprehension

Grades: Secondary

Lesson Objective/s:	To state the main idea of a paragraph using the RAP-Q strategy
Assessment/s:	Students will correctly state and apply the RAP-Q strategy to passage read
State Standards Correlation:	1.03 Demonstrate the ability to read, listen to, and view a variety of increasingly complex print and non-print expressive texts appropriate to grade level and course literary focus by demonstrating comprehension of main idea and supporting details
Materials/Resources:	A news article or short story of interest related to the Olympics past or present; Refer to James Madison Learning Toolbox (http://coe.jmu.edu/learningToolbox/rapq2.html) for history and science examples; hole-punched index cards
Preplanning Activities:	Choose a rap for opening (check carefully for appropriate content); Prepare advance organizer for lesson, post objective; Have the RAP strategy and a practice paragraph written on chart paper or projected onto screen. Have an independent practice paragraph ready for individual work

Lesson Element	Procedure for Teacher and Materials	Potential Barriers for Learning: The student has challenges with . . .	UDL Multiple Means of . . . • Representation • Engagement • Expression
Lesson Opening	Do you like to RAP? Objective: Today you will learn a strategy that will help you find the main idea of a paragraph.	Focusing/attention Motivation Language processing	Play a short RAP. Visually display objective and advance organizer on board. Provide advance organizer for lesson.
Teacher Input	Do you ever read something and wonder what it was you just read? The RAP-Q strategy can help you find the main idea of what you read. First, you read the paragraph. Next, you ask yourself questions. (What was this paragraph about? What were the main ideas?) Then, you put the main ideas in your own words.	Attention/motivation Making connections Processing Following directions	Use lots of expression. Vary loudness of voice to increase attention. Have RAP mnemonic strategy (provided at end of plan*) projected in room. Provide individual copies as needed. Students write strategy on index card and place on a ring with other strategies they use when they finish.

	Finally, ask yourself 3 Questions. Write these questions about the reading on an index card. Write the answers to the questions on the back of the cards. Teach students a catchy RAP-Q to remember the strategy. Have the words to the rap projected and practice. Project a practice paragraph and model how the strategy works.	Sequencing Articulation, fluency Stuttering Reluctant participant	Use transitional words in strategy presentation (first, next, then, finally, for example). Model RAP-Q "rap" and have students repeat each verse in unison after you model. Students may add a beat or rap sounds.
Guided Practice	Let's do the next paragraph together.	Processing Confidence	Provide multiple opportunities to practice.
Independent Practice	Introduce an article of interest about the Olympics past or present that is grade level appropriate. Have students read it on their own and apply the RAP-Q strategy. Write the main idea on an index card.	Following directions Recalling steps/organizing Comprehension Frustration	Have student repeat directions. Encourage students to use their visual models/strategy cards. Circulate while students are working, asking questions, offering constructive positive feedback. Praise good efforts.
Closure	Collect cards and ask students questions from their cards. Have students say or RAP the strategy before transitioning to next class/activity.	Confidence Remembering and understanding strategy	Praise students for their efforts. Be sure they keep their strategy rings in their notebooks. Remind them to use this strategy when they read.

Some students will apply the mnemonic to additional reading without prompting (**transfer of learning**).

Most students will correctly apply the mnemonic to express the main idea of a paragraph independently.

All students will identify the steps in the RAP-Q mnemonic strategy.

---

*RAP: Rap a Paragraph

First you take a paragraph and you read it, you read it. . . .
Rap a paragraph, Rap, Rap
Rap a paragraph, Rap, Rap

Next you ask yourself what was the main idea, idea . . .
Rap a paragraph, Rap, Rap
Rap a paragraph, Rap, Rap

Then you put it in your own words, your own words . . .
Rap a paragraph, Rap, Rap
Rap a paragraph, Rap, Rap

Then ask yourself 3 questions, 3 questions . . .
Rap a paragraph, Rap, Rap
Rap a paragraph, Rap, Rap

Sample Lesson Plans for Individuals With Hearing Impairments

7

7.1   Elementary: It's a Small World

7.2   Secondary: Olympic Locations

Sample Lesson Plan 7.1 It's a Small World

Area of Focus: Hearing Impaired

Subject: English Language Arts

Grades: K–1

Lesson Objective/s:	To read and comprehend text about different beliefs/cultures of people participating in the Olympics; To construct a flag using symbols that represent a country
Assessment/s:	Completed flags with expression of one or more country's values/beliefs
State Standards Correlation:	ELA 2.03 Read and comprehend both fiction and non-fiction text appropriate for grade one using: prior knowledge, summarizing, asking questions; 3.01 Elaborate on how information and events connect to life experiences; Social Studies: 1.03 Compare and contrast similarities and differences among individuals and families
Materials/Resources:	Book *People* by Peter Spier; an American flag, an Olympic flag (or picture of one); art supplies to make flags; pictures of different country flags (determine countries before lesson); recording of "It's a Small World"
Preplanning Activities:	Consult with specialist about individual needs (i.e., equipment needs, any need for sign language interpreter, for example); Prepare visual display of objective, advance organizer. If you have a co-teacher, have them create visuals for students to see as you teach

Lesson Element	Procedure for Teacher and Materials	Potential Barriers for Learning: The student has challenges with . . .	UDL Multiple Means of . . . • Representation • Engagement • Expression
Lesson Opening	Good morning, everyone! Hold up an American Flag. Ask what it represents. Hold up an Olympic flag or picture of one. Does anyone know what this flag represents? Objective: Today we are going to read about how people are the same and different.	Social interactions Student has moderate to severe hearing loss Activating prior knowledge Focusing Following lesson sequence	Be welcoming and positive. Teacher may use amplification device. Have student sit in front alongside peers. Teacher sits in usual place, away from noise sources (such as hallway). Use visuals to accompany speech. Using objects, visuals such as flags. Post objective on chart or board. Provide advance organizer.

Teacher Input	As we go through the book, be thinking about a flag you wish to create. You will be making a flag of a country when we finish reading. Read the book, *People* (by Peter Speir) with the class. Ask students what similarities and what differences they see among the world's people. List these on the board. Flags can show us what values and beliefs a country has. Hold up different flag models or pictures of country flags.	Hearing directions Physical placement in classroom sometimes Accessing oral reading of text/comments (often relies on seeing speaker's face)	Type basic directions so they can be seen. Allow student to move to another spot where he/she can hear better. Use document projector to share book if possible for full visual impact. Add gestures that help with meaning but try to keep hands from covering mouth. If there is another adult in the room, they could write student responses on a chart or board, adding a picture or symbol, etc.
Guided Practice	Demonstrate how to make a flag using provided art materials. Have different numbered work areas set up for different flags. Have children number off (1–4 if you have 4 stations) and then go to the station with that number.	Receiving oral directions Following procedures if only auditory cues provided	Try to stay in one place while demonstrating and face students. Have stations numbered. Try not to let the student feel singled out.
Independent Practice	Using pictures/models, students construct a flag of a different country. They may refer back to book, computer, or other resource to come up with additional symbols related to the beliefs/values of that country.	Accessing information auditorily Speaking in front of group	Provide templates, models, rulers, materials for flag construction. Rehearse the country's beliefs/values represented on flag with teacher or peer for response in closure.
Closure	Students share flags, explain the color/design, and express 2 or more values/beliefs of their country that the flag shows. How are our flags the same? How are they different? Sing "It's a Small World" and then wave flags.	Participating with group Getting cues from speaker May have alternate means of response Oral presentation of song	Add sign language/gestures. Be sure student with HI can see the teacher/leader. Allow verbal, sign language, or pictorial response. Have song lyrics on screen.

Some students will complete flag, express 2 or more beliefs, and research additional customs or traditions of that country.

Most students will complete flag, give 2 attributes, and express 2 representational values/beliefs.

All students will create a flag of a country, give 2 attributes (color, design), and express one belief or value that it represents.

Sample Lesson Plan 7.2 Olympic Locations

Area of Focus: Hearing Impairment

Subject: Geography

Grades: Secondary

Lesson Objective/s:	Examine the location trends of the Olympics (Winter or Summer) and compare to the most recent and predict other possible locations
Assessment/s:	Five proposed sites with rationale; Check with rubric
State Standards Correlation:	Social Studies: Examine the indicators of civilization, including writing, labor specialization, cities technology, trade, and political and cultural institutions
Materials/Resources:	Consult with a specialist to learn specific student needs/accommodations, any speech-to-text systems; laminated response cards and makers; computers with suggested websites for independent practice research or similar print materials/textbooks
Preplanning Activities:	Prepare PowerPoint with key text and questions, add visuals that help explain material; Bookmark a large world map to project or have one easily accessible in class

Lesson Element	Procedure for Teacher and Materials	Potential Barriers for Learning: The student has challenges with . . .	UDL Multiple Means of . . . • Representation • Engagement • Expression
Lesson Opening	Would our state be a likely location for the Olympics (Winter or Summer)? Why? Why not? Where have the last few Olympics been held? Objective: Today we will look at and identify criteria to evaluate locations for potential host cities/states for the Olympics.	Social interactions Student has moderate to severe hearing loss Activating prior knowledge Focusing Following lesson sequence	Be welcoming and positive. Teacher may use amplification device. Have student sit in front alongside peers (allow some choice). Teacher sits/stands in usual place, away from noise sources (such as hallway). Use print displays, other visuals, gestures to accompany speech (PowerPoint, perhaps a map reference here). Post objective on chart or board. Provide advance organizer/outline that includes clear directions for independent practice.
Teacher Input	What do you think is necessary geography to host a Winter (or Summer) Olympics? What other factors might influence a location that is selected?	Learning new vocabulary Attending Comprehending/accessing what is said/presented	Write any new words or key words on board. Be sure student is watching you. Rephrase questions if student doesn't respond correctly the first time.

	Activity	Concern	Accommodation
	Talk about other criteria/considerations that students did not mention.	Accessing information other students generate	List student responses on board or type into computer program that is being projected.
		Doesn't want to appear different from anyone else	Present criteria in PowerPoint (provide notes pages). Imbed key text into PowerPoint and add visuals when helpful. Imbed questions you are asking.
			Use a buddy to alert student to listen and be sure he/she understands (Think-Pair-Share or simply pausing after information is presented and buddies summarize what they learned).
			Encourage student to ask a friend who takes good notes to make a copy (let student with HI initiate).
Guided Practice	On a world map, mark the locations of all past and current Winter or Summer Olympic locations.	Receiving oral directions	Project a large world map.
			Point out locations while continuing to face student.
	What did these locations have in common? Let's make a list.	If speech is a problem . . .	Have students write responses with marker on laminated cards and hold up.
			Allow students to consult with another student before responding.
Independent Practice	Students take list of possible criteria that has been discussed and research different cities/countries. They are to make predictions of future possible sites based upon geography and other criteria.	Understanding directions	Refer to advance organizer.
			Have student repeat directions to you.
		Accessing information auditorily	Possible criteria is projected or listed on chart.
	Make your own list, include criteria and justification.		Maintain a class website for easy access to print materials that support any lectures/oral presentations.
		Hesitate to work in group	Provide some choice in grouping.
			Allow student to work alone.
Closure	Collect possible predicted sites and select the five most likely.	Speaking in front of group	Share written response with partners.
		Interacting with class	Display top five choices of class visually.
	Nice work today!		A classroom blog about the topics might also encourage peer interaction on the subject.
		Feeling comfortable in group	Offer encouragement, celebrate successes.

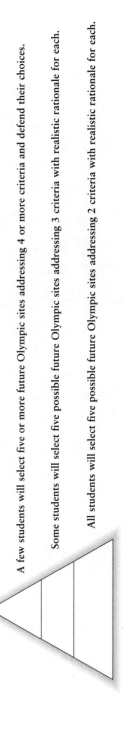

A few students will select five or more future Olympic sites addressing 4 or more criteria and defend their choices.

Some students will select five possible future Olympic sites addressing 3 criteria with realistic rationale for each.

All students will select five possible future Olympic sites addressing 2 criteria with realistic rationale for each.

Sample Lesson Plans for Individuals With Visual Impairments

8

Sample Lesson Plan 8.1   What Is Matter?

Area of Focus: Visual Impairments

Subject: Science

Grades: K–3

Lesson Objective/s:	To observe, describe the basic components of solids, liquids, and gas
Assessment/s:	Students clipboard data and responses in closure (teacher recording on checklist)
State Standards Correlation:	Matter: Solids, liquids, gas
Materials/Resources:	http://www.fossweb.com/modulesK–2/SolidsandLiquids/index.htmlwww.fossweb.com; recording/playing device (tape player, MP3, iPod), gather items for science introduction (items such as leaves, bubbles, water, ice, a rock, wool), chart paper and markers for tree map (masking tape and objects for tactile tree map if needed)
Preplanning Activities:	Keep doors completely closed, eliminate unnecessary obstacles from classroom so student can move about freely; Prepare objective/advance organizer in large print or as an audio recording (another student could do this); Pre-teaching of vocabulary can be done by another adult; Prepare reading materials in advance with VI teacher. Provide magnification devices if they work for the student(s); Alert students to procedures in case of emergency indoors or outdoors

Lesson Element	Procedure for Teacher and Materials	Potential Barriers for Learning: The student has challenges with . . .	UDL Multiple Means of . . . • Representation • Engagement • Expression
Lesson Opening	Students gather on carpet. What kind of weather do you observe at the Winter Olympics? Snow! Is snow a solid, a liquid, or a gas? Objective: Today we are going to observe and describe solids, liquids, and gases that we might see, hear, feel, touch, or taste at the Winter Olympics. We are even going to take our lesson outside today!	Orientation/time Identifying speakers Motivation Written schedules Procedures	Ring a bell for transitions. Pair with verbal directions. Have student sit near teacher and materials to be viewed; have a consistent place in the classroom for openings and presentations. Say names of students when you talk to them and when they respond. Have daily schedule and advance organizer recorded for easy access (or available in large print if that meets the learner needs). Review any procedures (raising hands, for example). Use a normal tone of voice with expression.
Teacher Input	Let's begin by reviewing our vocabulary words. Read audio books from www.fossweb.com (pair with visual book "Everything Matters") or show an auditorily descriptive video clip about matter.	Student may not see vocabulary in typical print	Preteach vocabulary (go through audio glossary at website: Solid, liquid, gas, matter, mixture, property [size, color, shape]). Allow time to talk about the meaning of each. Vocabulary cards can be provided that have large print, or Braille.

	Have leaves, bubbles, water, ice, a rock, and wool to demonstrate/feel the different properties. Let students feel each.	Accessing information by sight	Use audio books or used closed circuit television with videos.
			Provide tactile experiences with clear, explicit auditory descriptions.
	Tell students they are different and yet the same. How are they different? (Let students respond.) How are they the same?	Attending to questions	Keep an expressive tone of voice, continue to include student names. Praise efforts to respond and interact.
	They are all matter. There are 3 groups of matter. Can you name them? Yes, solids, liquids, and gas.	Remembering procedures	Remind students to raise hands if they can name them.
Guided Practice	Give students 3 response cards—one for solids, one for liquids, and one for gas. Show/feel some different examples and have them raise their card.	Student needs alternate means to receive information	Students each have 3 response cards with pictures for solid, liquid, or gas (have large print or Braille cards if needed)—students may work in teams (pair sighted student with student with VI).
Independent Practice	Go outside and identify different solids and liquids in the environment. Make a list on your clipboard. Return to classroom.	Mobility/Orientation	Pair students so sighted partners match up with students with VI. Instruct partner to do lots of descriptive talking while outside and be sure both students touch things they find. Be sure the items are safe. One person is the recorder and both people are "talkers" and "finders." Alert partner to watch for safety. Blow a whistle for students to assemble when it is time to come in.
Closure	Have a large tree map ready so students can share their findings and sort them according to solid, liquid, or gas. Ask students to provide a description of each.	Access to visual images / Time to plan and express responses	If student cannot see tree map, make an audio recording of their findings. Student may benefit from constructing a tactile tree map in an area near the one the teacher is writing on (made with tape on carpet/floor—student places objects in correct categories). Have students Think-Pair-Share with partner.

Some students will design an experiment to further analyze one or more properties of solids, liquids, and gases.

Most students will observe/identify two of each—solid, liquid, and gas—in their environment and give 2 properties of each.

All students will observe/identify a solid, liquid, and gas in their environment and give one property of each.

Sample Lesson Plan 8.2 Protecting Olympic Environments

Area of Focus: Visual Impairments—Secondary

Subject: Earth Science

Grade: 9

Lesson Objective/s:	Students will study the effects of population growth and development of land for the Winter Olympics
Assessment/s:	Audio recording of student responses
State Standards Correlation:	Evaluate water resources, storage and movement of groundwater, ecological services provided by the ocean and fresh water bodies, impacts of growing human population, natural and manmade contamination
Materials/Resources:	Trays, dirt, water, small plants, magazines, print sources for Vancouver
Preplanning Activities:	Keep doors completely closed, eliminate unnecessary obstacles from classroom so student can move about freely; Prepare objective/advance organizer in large print or as an audio recording (another student could do this); Pre-teaching of vocabulary can be done by another adult; Prepare reading materials in advance with VI teacher. Provide magnification devices if they work for the student(s); Alert students to procedures in case of emergency indoors or outdoors. Order recorded textbooks from Recordings for the Blind and dyslexic (www.rfd.org). Prepare websites/materials to be read aloud during independent practice. Check on computer-to-speech activation

Lesson Element	Procedure for Teacher and Materials	Potential Barriers for Learning: The student has challenges with . . .	UDL Multiple Means of . . . • Representation • Engagement • Expression
Lesson Opening	Demonstrate a mudslide down a barren and wet mountain slope using a tray, wet sand/dirt, and water. Tilt tray and add more water.	Conceptualizing need for forest growth, streams, influence of melting snow pack	Work with a sighted partner. Trays can be felt by hand and result from tipping trays. Speak in normal tone of voice with expression and enthusiasm.
	Objective: Today we are going to study the effects of population growth and development on the land used at the 2010 Winter Olympics in Vancouver.	Activating prior knowledge	
	Go over advance organizer and procedures for the lesson.	Motivation Written schedules Procedures	Have daily schedule, advance organizer, and any needed procedures recorded for easy access (or available in large print if that meets the learner needs). Review any procedures (raising hands, for example).
Teacher Input	What are the risks of deforestation to Whistler Blackcomb and Grouse Mountain? Identify factors that promote mudslides: • Overlogging • Past forest fires • Tree disease • Road/other development • Erosion	Acquiring new vocabulary	Pre-teach/present any new vocabulary with descriptive definitions. This could also be recorded for easy access.
		Identifying speakers	Say names of students when you talk to them and when they respond to aid orientation/comprehension.
		Accessing information visually	Use descriptive language when presenting information. Play a video clip about this subject that has descriptive audio on the computer or on closed circuit television.

		Accessing textbooks	Provide recorded textbook.
	Turn to your textbooks and look at pages xxxxx. As you read, see if you can answer this question: "What are the benefits of controlled growth?"		
Guided Practice	Add stability to sand/dirt tray. • What should be added? • What should be controlled? Compare amounts of standing water. Then drain standing water and compare.	Orientation of experiment Safely navigating through experiment Accidentally spilling water or sand	Work with a sighted partner on experiment. Activate tactile modalities. Instruct partner to use words to help with directionality: on your right/left, up/down, on the table near you, move forward/backward. Use time orientations for placement of materials relative to the student's position. ("The tray is on your table at 10 o'clock.") Be sure materials are stable.
Independent Practice	Search magazines, newspapers, internet on Vancouver's Olympic parks to learn how they protect their environment.	Finding and recording information	Research alone or with partner depending on comfort level and access to material that can be read aloud. Use computer text-to-speech features. Take notes with their Brailler, an electronic notetaker, computer, or tape recorder/MP3 player/iPod. If using computer, adjust color and contrast to meet student needs and enlarge font.
Closure	How do you think population growth and land development is being or can be controlled in Vancouver? What have you learned?	May need time to construct verbal response Note-taking	Discuss with partner before responding. Make audio recording of student responses that students can access. Be sure to include students' names in their responses.

Some students will research Vancouver's plan for population grown/land development and compile their findings.

Most students will complete assignment using adapted technology.

All students will tell/express one effect population growth and land development can have on an environment.

Sample Lesson Plans for Individuals With Physical Disabilities, Health Disabilities, and Related Low-Incidence Disabilities

9

Sample Lesson Plan 9.1   Let the Games Begin!

Area of Focus: Physical, Health, Low-Incidence

Subject: Physical Education

Grades: 4–8 (all students)—Can be easily adapted for primary

Lesson Objective/s:	To participate in a field day to celebrate the Olympic Spirit (Culminating Lesson)
Assessment/s:	Participation Checklists, Score Sheets/Recorded Times, distances recorded by homeroom teachers
State Standards Correlation:	Healthful Living 10.04 Work cooperatively and productively in a group to accomplish a set goal in both cooperative and competitive activities
Materials/Resources:	Flags of different countries, a cardboard torch with flashlight flame, paper origami doves, banners; All teachers, staff, parents, community volunteers
Preplanning Activities:	Work with coaches to make sure events are all physically accessible; PTs may be able to help obtain any needed adapted equipment. Meet with planning committee to review safety, other adaptations

Lesson Element	Procedure for Teacher and Materials	Potential Barriers for Learning: The student has challenges with . . .	UDL Multiple Means of . . . • Representation • Engagement • Expression
Lesson Opening	Begin with a processional of all the athletes for all students. Play Parade of Athletes music. Meet in gym or outdoor gathering area. Each class represents a different country and carries a representational flag.	Mobility (uses wheelchair)	Make sure hallways/entrances are clear/accessible. Allow students with physical needs to have an early start.
Teacher Input	• Principal or other leader opens the Games • Light a torch • Raise the Olympic Flag (Play "Olympic Hymn") • Students take turns telling highlights of the first Olympics • Everyone says the Olympic Oath • Release paper doves • "Let the Games Begin"	Having leadership roles in school Communication	Plan for students in this category to have some leadership roles . . . raising Olympic flag, carrying torch, lighting flame, for example. Plan for any needed adaptations or physical supports in advance. Rehearse Olympic Oath ahead of time. Program into communication devices. Program switches that say "Let the Games Begin." Make banners that say "Let the Games Begin" to hold up.

Guided Practice	Students go with their homeroom teachers to assigned events that are run by other teachers, parents, community volunteers and rotate through events.	Safety	Alert adults/helpers to any health-related problems that might occur and have plans in place in case they are needed.
Independent Practice	Students rotate through events such as: • Shot Put • Relay races • Hurdles • Basketball Shoot • Olympic Rings Extension: Have students pre-plan by researching and creating flags, making paper doves, and reading "Sadako and the Paper Cranes"; write a news release about the event.	Mobility	Have students move with buddy or adult staff member or volunteer.
			Participate in event with a buddy.
		Manipulating equipment	Provide adapted equipment as needed.
			Modify requirements of event as needed.
		Communication	Pre-program any augmentative communication devices such as *Go Talks* to help students communicate with others as they navigate through the events.
		Response time	Allow students extra time to complete their event.
		Fatigue	Plan for frequent breaks.
			Students who are able to use their hands to fold but have low physical stamina otherwise can make paper origami cranes for release.
Closure	• Students return to initial gathering area. • Students sit by their country flag. • The Greek flag is raised as the Greek anthem is played. • Certificate packets with gold stickers are presented to all teachers for distribution in class. • Carry out Olympic flag while playing "Olympic Spirit."	Mobility	Allow students in wheelchairs to enter early.
		Being isolated from peers	Arrange for their country spaces to be on the sides so they can sit with their peers.
		Self-confidence/Pride	Display certificate in a special place. Add a picture of student participating in events.

Some students will have a leadership role in the opening and closing ceremonies or help prepare for it.

Most students will complete five events in the allotted time.

All students will participate in the field day events and receive a certificate.

Sample Lesson Plan 9.2 Technology Changes Over Time

Area of Focus: Physical Disabilities

Subject: Physical Science

Grade: 8

Lesson Objective/s:	Describe the technology and the physical principles that have changed snow skiing from wood to present-day materials
Assessment/s:	Group data/poster display and explanations with rubric
State Standards Correlation:	Evaluate technological designs for application of scientific principles, risks and benefits, constraints of design, consistent testing protocols
Materials/Resources:	Skis (real or picture), ACC Devices (as needed), laptop with enlarged keyboard (The student may already have these kinds of devices and have assistance with them)
Preplanning Activities:	Collect skis or pictures of skis (student with physical disability may assist preparing by downloading pictures from the computer), video clips/books with visuals of different kinds of skiing, have any websites programmed for access by using one switch; Have poster template and directions for constructing posted in room or on tables/desks

Lesson Element	Procedure for Teacher and Materials	Potential Barriers for Learning: The student has challenges with . . .	UDL Multiple Means of . . . • Representation • Engagement • Expression
Lesson Opening	List all sports that have had equipment made from wood and have changed to other materials as a result of technology.	Attention Communication Mobility	Show a picture of a wooden ski and one made today. Pre-record or activate alternative communication devices if needed for participation (most students will not need). Be sure classroom is arranged for easy access by wheelchairs and that all needed materials are within reach. Adjust table heights as needed. Consider providing slantboards and paper or book holders if appropriate.
Teacher Input	Discuss Olympic events requiring skis. • How are the events different? • What do the skis all have in common? • What might make them different? Teacher fills in a Venn Diagram or double bubble map with responses.	Background knowledge Positioning Formulating verbal, written, or physical responses Needs structure	If students are not familiar with snow skis, try to bring some real ones. Show a video clip of different type of Olympic and other skiing events. Try to include one of a person with a physical disability skiing. Be sure student is comfortable with positioning and can see/hear everything. Allow wait time for responses. Provide advance organizer. Use graphic organizers to organize content.

Guided Practice	Students work in groups and ask these questions regarding different skiing events. Guide students toward poster display of findings, beginning with • Internet search • Group by design changes, material changes, technique changes	Difficulty speaking Organization Takes extra time to provide responses Needs adaptations to access internet Limited fine motor control for writing or drawing on poster	Student may use an augmentative communication (ACC) device or computer with text to speech capabilities. Keep vocabulary current and updated. Have clear, written directions of poster creation. Have a sample of a template for reference in poster creation. Demonstrate. Work with peers to allow wait time. Allow student to use laptop with any switches, enlarged keyboards/overlays as needed. Have some helpful internet sites accessible with one key stroke if needed. Student can type or download pictures/words and type short phrases for poster display.
Independent Practice	Students group data and display on poster boards for presentation. Evaluate what technology has affected: • Faster times, longer distances • How skis adapt to changes • Changes to events *Extended practice:* Students can research other types of equipment with evolving technology that they have a personal interest in. They can investigate physical science principles that apply to these changes.	Difficulty graphically presenting and constructing poster board Writing Fatigue Speaking Feeling isolated from peers in sports or other area or simply wanting to participate	Students may graph data using a computer graphing program (Microsoft Excel, for example) and add graph to poster. Students may speak/record or type their evaluative findings. Allow for breaks. Group can record findings to present to group. Student can research a technology adaptation that might help them participate in a sport or other activity in his/her own life.
Closure	Describe physical science principles that apply to these technology changes.	Difficulty speaking	Play audio recording made with group to describe physical science principles. Show poster with graph.

Some students will research other types of sports equipment in the same way—by evaluating data collected and analyzing physical science principles that apply to these changes.

Most students will analyze the physical science principles that apply to these technology changes using data they have graphed.

All students will compare and contrast the technology and physical principles of ski equipment over the years and tell how it benefits today's skiers.

Sample Lesson Plans for Individuals Who Are Gifted and Talented

10

Sample Lesson Plan 10.1   Friendship Quilt

Area of Focus: Gifted & Talented

Subject: Mathematics, Social Studies, Visual Arts

Grades: Elementary (3)

Lesson Objective/s:	To construct a quilt square that represents Olympic friendships using technology
Assessment/s:	Completed square with student expression of meaning
State Standards Correlation:	3.02 Describe the change in attributes as two- and three-dimensional figures are cut and rearranged. 1.05 Use area or region models and set models of fractions to explore part-whole relationships. 2.01 Select and use appropriate features and functions of hardware and software for class assignments. 3.13 Use his/her own ideas and feelings when creating artwork
Materials/Resources:	KWL chart, 6 x 6 cotton squares (1 per student) and felt for pattern cut-outs or 6 x 6 paper squares with multi-colored construction paper for pattern cut-outs; rulers, scissors, glue; invite a parent or community member to assist with lesson if possible (and perhaps bring a quilt or two)
Preplanning Activities:	Secure computer lab if needed, be familiar with paint program

Lesson Element	Procedure for Teacher and Materials	Potential Barriers for Learning: The student has the need to . . .	UDL Multiple Means of . . . • Representation • Engagement • Expression
Lesson Opening	Hold up a quilt and ask what students know about quilts/record responses on KWL chart. We have been asked by the school planning committee to design and display a quilt that represents the Olympics. Our task is to construct a quilt that represents the feelings of friendships represented by the Olympics as well as in our school community.	Connect to community and create Engage in problem-based learning Engage sense of idealism	Hold up a quilt, have books on quilts displayed (including children's books); have a community quilter share some quilts. Have some books on the Olympics displayed. Connect learning to community needs and activities.
Teacher Input	Quilters use mathematics to design the geometric shapes of their quilts as they tell their stories. Point out some of the patterns/arrays on the quilt, in the books, or projected on the computer. Point out any appliqués on the quilt squares. Talk about the use of color and what colors complement each other.	Appeal to intellectual curiosity Engage spatial and mathematical senses (discovering patterns/relationships) Develop creativity	Show different quilt designs that reflect simple geometric designs to more complex and abstract. Show video clip or projected web sources or have quilter "anchor" the lesson and present this kind of information. Bring in visual art principles about primary, secondary, complimentary colors.

Guided Practice	Demonstrate the design of a quilt square using a computer paint program. Demonstrate how this design can be printed out and used as a template. Show students how they can add appliqués to personalize designs on the squares.	Rapid learning pace Be creative, express sense of self	One demonstration should be enough. However, steps may be written down or on a video for reference as needed. Student designs appliqué.
Independent Practice	Students will explore bookmarked internet sites and/or available books to investigate quilt patterns. Students will choose a design to create a square that reflects the colors and feelings of the Olympics/friendships. They will express why they chose a particular design. Ask one student to create a square with the Olympic rings. Have students sign and date their squares using a permanent thin-lined marker. Extension: Why do you think there are so many children's books that reference quilting? Why do they often also relate to friendship themes?	Allow time for exploration Works well independently Allow choice To make a personal connection with the art May complete work quickly Needs even greater (or different) challenge	Students may use a computer paint program to design a square and print it out. Record why they choose a particular pattern on an index card. Allow them to make multiple squares. Explore the children's books displayed that are on quilting and record a commentary on it.
Closure	Place quilt squares together. Place a square with the Olympic Rings in the center. Ask students what mathematical connections they observe in their completed projects. Ask students how this quilt reflects the feelings of Olympic friendships. Display quilt in building.	Seeing parts come together to make a whole Higher-level thinking/elaboration Express feelings of empathy and idealism Express feeling of contributing to whole community	Assemble quilt together. Students express why they chose a particular pattern, design, and/or colors for their quilt square and how it reflects Olympic friendship.

Some students will examine a set of children's books on quilting and record a commentary on themes they find in the stories.

Most students will tell why they chose their pattern, design, and colors for their quilt square and how it reflects Olympic friendship.

All students will create one quilt square using technology and express one or more attributes of it.

Sample Lesson Plan 10.2   The Cost of the Olympics

Area of Focus: Gifted and Talented

Subject: Economics

Grades: 9–12

Lesson Objective/s:	To learn, apply, and debate the concept of cost-benefit analysis to the Winter or Summer Olympics
Assessment/s:	Completed spreadsheet and debate presentation with rubric
State Standards Correlation:	4.04 Recognize and analyze value upon which judgments are made
Materials/Resources:	Computers, pictures/symbols of Olympics in background or projected
Preplanning Activities:	Arrange to use the computer lab or order laptop cart, prepare advance organizer; List some helpful websites that students can access easily

Lesson Element	Procedure for Teacher and Materials	Potential Barriers for Learning: The student has the need to . . .	UDL Multiple Means of . . . • Representation • Engagement • Expression
Lesson Opening	Have images of the most recent Olympics projected on the screen as students enter room.	Be highly engaged	Tap into possible interest areas.
	If the Summer Olympics came to our city for two weeks, what would we need to be prepared to host it?	Engage in problem-based learning	Pose a question (What . . . if?).
	Objective: Today we will apply the concept of cost-benefit analysis to a city hosting the Summer (or Winter) Olympics.	To see purpose in what they do	State and post objective.
	Advance Organizer:	Use time wisely and plan	Show and post advance organizer.
	✓ Review cost and benefit ✓ Set up spreadsheet and basic list ✓ Research internet to improve list ✓ Share results ✓ Debate value of holding next Olympics in your city/state		
Teacher Input	What is meant by cost and by benefit?	Engage in questioning at a variety of levels	Refer to Bloom's taxonomy to generate questions.
	Are costs and benefits always measureable by dollars?		
	Do benefits happen only during events?		
	How can we compare costs and benefits?		

Guided Practice	Have students set up a table/spreadsheet to compare costs and benefits for the most recent Summer (or Winter) Olympics.	Students may set their tables up as teacher models	May prefer facilitated instruction.
		Work at own pace	Allow for differences in pacing.
		Infuse technology	To increase and/or capitalize on technology skills.
Independent Practice	Research internet to improve list of costs and benefits. Find data appropriate for costs and benefits.	Working independently	May work alone.
		Classifying/seeing relationships	Students organize data in spreadsheet and refer to a textbook to generate their conclusions.
	Analyze findings and prepare for debate. Print out completed spreadsheet for upcoming debate.	Students need extra challenge or prefer another method of engagement response	Student could work with partner who is constructing spreadsheet and use that data to pre-write arguments for the essay (allow word processor or handwriting).
	Extension: Write a persuasive essay about why the Olympics should be held in your city or another city in your state.		
Closure	Debate value of holding the next Olympics in the city you have researched.	Use verbal skills	Use rubric to assess debate. Collect and assess spreadsheets.

Some students will compose a persuasive essay about why the Olympics should be held in their city or state. Data analysis must support their arguments.

Most students will collect and organize their data in a spreadsheet and prepare 2 or 3 argument statements for the closing debate.

All students will collect and display data that reflects the costs and benefits of holding the Olympics. They will prepare one argument statement to present in the closing debate.

About the Author

Debbie Metcalf currently works in partnership with Pitt County Schools and East Carolina University in Greenville, North Carolina. She is an Intervention Specialist for Pitt County Schools and serves as a Teacher-in-Residence in the Department of Curriculum and Instruction at East Carolina University. She teaches methods courses and works in the classroom with undergraduate pre-service teachers. Debbie received a Master of Arts in Education degree from San Diego State University and is certified in both general and special education, including assistive technology. She became a National Board Certified Teacher in 1997. In 2004, she was awarded the Clarissa Hug Teacher of the Year Award from the International Council for Exceptional Children.

Debbie has taught students of all ages for over 30 years in California, New Mexico, Hawaii, Michigan, and North Carolina. She continues to mentor new teachers and teachers pursuing National Board Certification. Her primary research areas include access to the general curriculum for students with exceptionalities, collaborative teaching models, alternative assessment models for diverse learners, curriculum revision, alignment, and service learning.

Supporting researchers for more than 40 years

Research methods have always been at the core of SAGE's publishing program. Founder Sara Miller McCune published SAGE's first methods book, *Public Policy Evaluation*, in 1970. Soon after, she launched the *Quantitative Applications in the Social Sciences* series—affectionately known as the "little green books."

Always at the forefront of developing and supporting new approaches in methods, SAGE published early groundbreaking texts and journals in the fields of qualitative methods and evaluation.

Today, more than 40 years and two million little green books later, SAGE continues to push the boundaries with a growing list of more than 1,200 research methods books, journals, and reference works across the social, behavioral, and health sciences. Its imprints—Pine Forge Press, home of innovative textbooks in sociology, and Corwin, publisher of PreK–12 resources for teachers and administrators—broaden SAGE's range of offerings in methods. SAGE further extended its impact in 2008 when it acquired CQ Press and its best-selling and highly respected political science research methods list.

From qualitative, quantitative, and mixed methods to evaluation, SAGE is the essential resource for academics and practitioners looking for the latest methods by leading scholars.

For more information, visit **www.sagepub.com**.